ISFJ: Understanding & Relating with the Protector

MBTI Personality Types Series

By: Clayton Geoffreys

Table of Contents

Foreword

Have you ever been curious about why you behave certain ways? Well I know I have always pondered this question. When I first learned about psychology in high school, I immediately was hooked. Learning about the inner workings of the human mind fascinated me. Human beings are some of the most impressive species to ever walk on this earth. Over the years, one thing I've learned from my life experiences is that having a high degree of self-awareness is critical to get to where you want to go in life and to achieve what you want to accomplish. A person who is not self-aware is a person who lives life blindly, accepting what some label as fate. I began intensely studying psychology to better understand myself, and through my journey, I discovered the Myers Brigg Type Indicator (MBTI), a popular personality test that distinguishes between sixteen types of individuals. I hope to cover some of the most prevalent personality types of the MBTI test and share my findings with you through a series of books. Rather than just reading this for the sake of reading it though, I want you to reflect on the information that will be shared with you. Hopefully from reading *ISFJ: Understanding & Relating with the Protector*, I can pass along some of the abundance of information I have learned about ISFJs in general, how they view the world, as well as their greatest strengths and weaknesses. Thank you for purchasing my book. Hope you enjoy and if you do, please do not forget to leave a review! Also, check out my website at claytongeoffreys.com to join my exclusive list where I let you know about my latest books. To thank you for your purchase, you can go to my site to download a free copy of *33 Life Lessons: Success Principles, Career Advice & Habits of Successful People*. In the book, you'll learn from some of the greatest thought leaders of different industries on what it takes to become successful and how to live a great life.

Cheers,

Clayton Geoffreys

An Introduction to MBTI

Are you an introvert or an extrovert? It is a hot topic lately, with new books being written every year about the "power of introverts," as well as advice on how to thrive in an extrovert's world. In the workplace particularly, employers are finally realizing that paying attention to differences in the working styles of personality types can make or break a project.

It is true that the two types could not be more different if they tried. Introverts are seen as quiet, meek souls who are more likely to prefer that Friday nights spent at home alone with a good book. On the other side of the scale, extroverts are often take-charge types who need their workdays and weekends to be full of both action and people.

To many, the comparisons of "quiet" versus "outgoing" have been seen as too simple to adequately describe these personality traits. For this reason, the concepts of introversion and extroversion have been dissected and discussed in the psychology field for many years, with entire research journals devoted to the topic. The two words come from a theory by a psychologist named Carl Jung, who studied personality types. Jung looked at all of the different ways in which we behave and realized that there was a common thread that linked many of them. Isabel Myers-Briggs and her mother continued his work, with the result being the creation of the Myers-Briggs test. Their goal was to create a test that translated Jung's more complex concepts into those that could be understood by the everyday person.[1]

Test takers often report understanding themselves and the decisions they make better after receiving their scores. Communication styles and values are highlighted in these scores as well, which can lead to a better dynamic between co-workers and improved teamwork in the workplace.[2]

The test itself consists of questions that categorize and score the methods we use to make our everyday decisions. There are four dimensions that are scored and these, along with those all-important concepts of introversion and extroversion, help to label a person as one of sixteen possible personality types.[3]

The Four Dimensions of the MBTI

Here is a scenario: Your employer wants you to move to another state so that they can set up a new office in the area. You would have to uproot your family and live in a place that you have only visited once or twice before. Before leaving the office, your boss informs you that they will need your decision by next week. How would you make this choice? While some would use logic to determine their next step, others would need their choice to simply "feel right." On the Myers-Briggs test, each of these people would be categorized as preferring "sensing" or "intuition" respectively.

As mentioned earlier, there are four dimensions on the test that look at how we make decisions and embrace our lives.

First, let's look at introversion and extroversion. This is the probably the most well-known dimension from the test. You will be defined as an introvert (I) if you are the type who prefers to rely on yourself and the environment around you for your energy. You find ideas and concepts interesting and enjoy your solitude and privacy.[4] Others may describe you as 'shy', although it may or may not be accurate.

Extroverts (E) draw their energy from other people and objects. If this is you, it is more likely that you need much more stimulation and action in your life than an introvert would. After being in the middle of a crowd or mingling for an extended period of time, you may find that you feel energized. When describing you, others might use the word 'sociable'.[5]

Sensing vs. Intuition describes how someone makes sense of the world around them. As a sensing (S) test-taker, you discover information through your five senses. You prefer to rely on facts for your decisions, often have an excellent memory, and live in the present moment.[6]

If your scores indicate that you use intuition (I), this means that you focus on possibilities, as opposed to realities, and may report having a "hunch" about something when asked to explain yourself. Most people who are defined this way are imaginative and focused on the future.[7]

Feeling vs. Thinking is self-explanatory. Belonging in the category of feeling (F) means that your personal morals and emotions sway the decision-making process. You favor harmony and will let its potential presence guide you, indicating that you may be more subjective and tactful than most.[8]

If you have a preference for the thinking (T) trait, you can interpret this to mean that you allow past experiences to color your present decisions. You rely on logic and can be very analytical and objective.[9]

Judgment vs. Perception is the function people use when viewing the outside world. Preferring closure when it comes to your decisions categorizes you as someone who is Judging (J). You may use either logic or feelings during the process and you are often described as organized and determined.[10]

Scoring the highest in the Perceiving (P) category is likely to identify you as curious and spontaneous. Before making a decision (which can take quite a while), you will consider all possibilities. The right decision is one that can be changed if needed.[11]

Why is the Myers-Briggs Type Indicator Significant?

With the test results from the Myers-Briggs, we can get a better understanding of how our thought processes, as well as those of others, work. While many personality tests simply provide us with a list of traits that we do or do not possess, the Myers-Briggs is more thorough in describing the nuances that exist in people through their sixteen personality types. In essence, the test can help us understand who we are, an aspect that is particularly helpful when it comes to communicating with and working alongside others.[12] The effectiveness of the test has also been validated through years of research. These elements combine to set the Myers-Briggs apart from other personality tests.

When you understand the differences between the types, the results become even more significant. In these situations, knowing your type and that of others can enhance communication in essentially any sort of relationship. This is one reason why the test is becoming so popular in the workplace. Imagine being able to create a productive team with members who understand how their colleagues think and are able to bounce ideas off of each other seamlessly? Moreover, a better grasp of type differences could lead to more effective conflict resolution during those inevitable circumstances when they disagree. In the personal relationship arena, many have noticed that romance is more likely to last between certain types. An introverted, intuitive person is more likely to enjoy the company of another intuitive person, even if they are extroverted. You can also use the test results to gain insight into your significant other's quirks.[13] The utility of this test is far-reaching in all of these cases, in addition to other facets of our personal lives.

The Myers-Briggs test has also proved its usefulness in the career and education arenas. The four letters that make up your type provide information about your preferences, with the two middle letters having particular significance for the career(s) you are most likely to enjoy. For example, if your middle letters are NF (intuition + feeling) you are more likely to be idealistic and may enjoy a career in a helping field. Conversely, if your letters are ST (sensing + thinking), you may find that you prefer an occupation with more rules and regulations, such as a police officer or librarian.[14] The learning process can also be deciphered with the test.

In terms of education, there are many factors at play. As an introverted student, you will most likely prefer to work alone, while group work is usually more enticing to extroverts. Students who are thinking or sensing have been noted to prefer clear and organized lectures, while intuitive students may enjoy learning about a general theory, rather than its details.[15]

It is clear that the results of the Myers-Briggs test can be generalized to more settings and conditions than many other personality tests. Learning about your type can provide you with information that can be used to develop beneficial relationships and experience growth as an individual.

Uncovering the "Protectors": Who is an ISFJ?

It has been estimated that ISFJ's make up about 10% of the population.[16] As an ISFJ, your personality is without equal among the Myers-Briggs types in several ways. Firstly, although you are an Introvert (I), you also have the well-developed social skills of an Extrovert (E). In addition, your Feeling (F) trait does not prevent you from using logic when needed, much like someone who normally uses Thinking (T). Furthermore, as a Judging (J) type, you have the ability to make decisions quickly. However, you are also open to new ideas, provided that a detailed reason and plan are given for the change. This quality is more common to Perceptive (P) types.[17] Your unique personality is often granted the ability to get along with all types of people.

ISFJ's are among the several Myers-Briggs personality types who strive to provide service to others in their daily lives. Unlike other types who enjoy supplying this assistance, you do it because you feel that it is your duty as a human being.[18] When providing this help, you favor ministering to individual needs instead of the wants of a group. Furthermore, you are often drawn to those who are the most disadvantaged. You are also unlikely to take up a divisive cause, due to your preference for upholding traditional social conventions.[19] In fact, tradition has a place in almost all areas of your life, including your jobs, friendships, and other personal relationships.

With that said, when it comes to partaking in life's pleasures, your self-restraint is legendary. After meeting an ISFJ, it quickly becomes obvious that this is the type of person who believes that play must be earned. Still, while you are devoted to your work, your personal relationships are most important to you, particularly when it comes to those that are romantic or familial.

At work, as well as in most other parts of your life, you are determined, organized, and detail-oriented. Although your dedication often makes you an essential employee to your organization, the reluctance you have to demand recognition can lead to a lack of appreciation for your work. This experience can be common at home as well and the ISFJ may need to discover the value of speaking up.[20]

In general, you learn best by trying things out yourself, instead of reading from a book or studying a theory. During this process, you will also prefer using facts to solve any problems that may arise. This type is also a fan of using any refined skills that they have picked up in their occupation as well.

Routine is pleasant to the ISFJ, as are rules and structure. You expect that those close to you will follow societal rules without being told and can become embarrassed if this does not happen. However, as you age, you may become more relaxed and regard such behavior as an oddity. In any case, your excellent social skills make you adept at defusing any tension present in these situations.

As an ISFJ, it is likely that you are popular among many. This is partially due to your skill in reading others' emotions. Your excellent memory also plays a part in that it allows you to keep track of the special occasions and likes of many. When attending events, your gifts are always well received, thanks to your insight and natural inclination towards generosity.[21]

Your popularity can have a dark side however, particularly since you prefer to have only a few, close friends. This is often due to the fact that you are incredibly sensitive and need to share a deep bond with your companions. Due to this and aversion to any type of conflict, you may have a lot of difficulty saying no and can even suffer from psychosomatic illnesses. A short retreat to your home or other space in which you are most comfortable to "recharge" can help to remedy this issue.

Due to your well-developed sense of aesthetics, your home is likely to be cozy and tastefully decorated. Your organizational skills will also ensure that it is spotless, with everything in its correct place at all times. Your home life follows the same path in that your spouse and children never lack for care physically or emotionally.[22]

The personality traits of the ISFJ combine to form someone who is kind, dependable, and nurturing. You are known for putting forth your best effort regardless of the circumstance and this attribute is among the many that make you a wonderful partner, friend, and leader.

Why are ISFJs Indispensable Leaders?

When most people think of an effective leader, they think of an assertive type, with the ability to delegate tasks to those who can complete them most effectively. Charisma and a risk-taker are qualities sure to be on the list as well. However, what about someone who is quiet yet committed to the project at hand and its team members' happiness? These qualities are characteristic of an ISFJ and they are part of what makes you a great leader. Although you may not volunteer for the spotlight, your natural need to succeed will lead to accomplishments in many areas.

Even though you are not considered to be intuitive, you usually have great skill in "reading" the emotions of the people you work with and often get along quite well with them. Your exceptional memory skills can also be a boon, especially since they can help you discern what works well and what does not when it comes to fostering the dynamic between others.

As mentioned before, an ISFJ can be very committed to the task at hand or the cause they have taken up. Once you have set a goal it can be very difficult, if not impossible, to distract or discourage you from your path. Objectives that will improve the lives of others are of particular interest to you. It is important to note that, in general, you are extremely humble and will not seek widespread recognition for your accomplishments. ISFJ's simply want to know that whomever they have helped is living a better life.[23] Nevertheless, you are also down-to-earth and realistic, qualities that can be very helpful when it comes to leading others. These characteristics also ensure that you will carefully consider any and all relevant facts before you make a decision.

When planning, you always seem to know exactly what you need to do and how much you need to spend in order to get the best outcome. There is no doubt that your superb organizational and financial skills make this task much easier than it would be for another type. No detail is too small for you to notice and this capacity for being detail-oriented means that you will complete the more tedious tasks that others would prefer to ignore. Any instructions you give are sure to be clear and comprehensive and you can be sure that every person who works for you will know what they are expected to accomplish, along with any deadlines or other important information.

As an ISFJ leader, you also ensure that any necessary meetings start and end on time and that relevant issues are actually discussed, as well as possible solutions. It can definitely be said that you lead by example, often working long hours after everyone else has quit or is taking a break. However, you also care about work-family balance for both yourself and your subordinates. At work, if an employee needs to leave the office early or for a few hours, you won't be bothered. In fact, you love harmony and will strive to keep a pleasant working environment for everyone. You do this because both giving and inspiring loyalty is very important to you. For these reasons you are often described as a thoughtful and caring leader whose strong moral compass allows you to see what is right versus wrong when it comes to both your actions and the actions of others.[24]

Since ISFJ's truly enjoy working and serving others, they make wonderful candidates for leadership. Your ability to care for others, combined with your discipline and natural need to follow through are among the many strengths of your type.

The 7 Greatest Strengths of an ISFJ

Each of the Myers-Briggs personality types has their own gifts that make them a valuable member of society. Being aware of your strengths is only the first step in the process of personal development, however. As you cultivate these talents, you will find that you are provided with many more opportunities that will allow you to discover your true potential.

1. Work Ethic is Extraordinary

Your tendency to become attached to a cause, person, or organization means that you have no problem committing yourself to the completion of a project.[25] Concentrating on a task for long periods of time is almost easy for you, thanks to your introversion and thirst for knowledge. It is precisely this interest in ideas that keeps you from feeling as though you are missing out on the world around you in the moments when you are hunched over a desk. Any opportunity you have to practice the skills and strategies you have learned is enjoyable to you as well. Of course, it also helps that you view work as a duty and a virtue, instead of an option.

2. Exceptional Memory

An ISFJ's ability to store information about people they meet and situations of value is one reason they are so well liked. When you use this talent at work, you can quickly become the MVP of your team. You are the retail employee who remembers every customer's name and what they bought the last time they came in. In the office, you can remember the details and specifications from your reports, saving everyone some much-needed time. Your talent for recollection also comes in handy with your children and spouses, as you can often recall the little details that make them feel special.

3. Everyone Can Depend on You

Your type is extremely dependable, something you take much pride in. You make sure that you meet every deadline and are present at every recital or spelling bee. In fact, your well-being is sometimes contingent on this responsible and capable reputation. The more accomplished and talented you appear, the higher your self-esteem is. This means that putting in any extra time and effort is always worth it to you.

4. Committed to Relationships

Although you value all personal relationships, the amount of time a person has been in your life is important to you. The ISFJ prefers long-term romantic relationships and values the closeness that can be found in established friendships. Because of this, you have no problem working toward maintaining these connections once you have decided they are worth it. You also show your appreciation at work by giving your personal loyalty to professional contacts you

26

respect. In some cases, it is not uncommon for you to follow such a person to another job.

5. Support is Almost Guaranteed

No one can say that you have any qualms when it comes to sharing your knowledge and experience with others. You will do the same with your time and energy as well, particularly when it comes to those you are close to. Your self-image and empathy guide you to the position of confidante and advice giver more often than not.[26] Stability can be found in your presence and this type of support is almost always available with no expectations or conditions on your part. Since they yearn for the same treatment from their loved ones in their own lives, the ISFJ is able to fulfill this role very well. During those rare occasions when you find yourselves disagreeing with someone, you can remedy the situation fairly quickly by compromising.

6. Ability to See Right from Wrong

The moral compass that you possess is considered to be very strong. ISFJ's are quite capable of perceiving how to make the world more balanced and will strive for harmony in all situations. Your imagination allows you to consider the perspectives of others and you are truly fascinated by your peers.[27] The talent you have for identifying exactly what others love or can tolerate is enhanced by the aforementioned skill.

7. Innate Need to Help and Protect

The last strength of an ISFJ is its need to help protect and provide. Seen as part of your responsibility as a human being, you will go out of your way to provide comfort and/or physical necessities, particularly to those who come from a disadvantaged background. Your enthusiasm when it comes to your altruism cannot be dampened. Part of this is due to the fact that you have an emotional connection to the cause or people you care for. Whatever the reason, there are only a few Myers-Briggs personalities who have the sort of dedication that you possess when it comes to the betterment of society.

The 5 Greatest Areas of Improvement for an ISFJ

The strengths that you possess are almost too numerous to count. Your thoughtfulness and willingness to serve carves a unique place among other Myers-Briggs types. Still, some of your tendencies and attitudes often have a part in the unhealthy situations you may find yourself in. In improving some of the mindsets and approaches that are common to all ISFJ's, you may find that your ability to accomplish your goals is considerably enhanced.

1. Counting Humility as a Virtue

In your opinion, hard work is and should be expected in our daily lives. The work of many can prevent societal collapse and inspire a greater future. This is something that we all want, even if we are not willing to share the burden of making it happen. Therefore, calling attention to the accomplishments that stem from this work is somewhat vulgar. You believe that this is the case no matter the situation and regardless of what was sacrificed. So why do you feel so frustrated or annoyed when you are passed up for that promotion that you know you were qualified for? If you had mentioned a few of the times that you *had* been there for that friend, would you still be fighting? It is worth reconsidering just how much your modesty helps you grow personally and professionally in your life.

2. Perceiving Conflict as Terrifying

It is no secret that ISFJ's hate confrontation. You will often go to extreme lengths to be there for a friend, no matter how much it may inconvenience you. Just the potential of making others angry or upset can make you feel trapped when it comes to figuring out what to say. The fact that you shoulder almost all of the responsibility for the dynamics in the relationships in your life certainly doesn't help. Saying no to others (as well as to yourself) may make your worrying go into hyper-drive, but it doesn't have to be this way. Learning to prepare for and resolve conflict peacefully can do wonders for your self-esteem and your health.

3. Accepting Those "New Fangled Notions"

Traditions are there for a reason. Your mentality is that if it worked well in the past, it should work just as well in the present, with very few exceptions. While this notion may be true, you should keep in mind that the fact that it works does not mean that there are not better ways of doing it. Perhaps that project that took you three weeks to finish could have been completed in half that time if you had used that new method your supervisor mentioned. The idea of changing the rules is something you have an aversion to, particularly if there is no "good" reason for it. Opening up your mind to realms outside of the traditional can go a long way in improving your life in many areas.

4. Believe Spontaneity Does Not Equal Out of Control

More often than not, your life is organized down to the day and possibly to the hour or minute. To say that your type could learn to be a little more spontaneous is an understatement. Even your vacations are planned out to the max, as you want to fit in as much sightseeing as you can. Still, being prepared for everything is not always possible and this can be a very hard lesson to learn. You may not ever find yourself yearning for a surprise, but accepting their potential presence in your life can allow you to experience and enjoy life in a way that you never have before.

5. Repressing Your Feelings

Your type has an extremely hard time letting out their feelings. This is mostly due to your sensitivity and worrying about how others will react to it. What is ironic is that the outcome of holding in your emotions can often have a worse effect than it would have if you had let them out in the first place. Verbally lashing out at those you care about, excessive muscle tension and anxiety will be a consistent part of your life if you choose not to pay attention to this issue.

As mentioned before, your strengths more than outnumber your weaknesses. If you focus on these five areas for improvement, there is even the possibility that you can modify them in such a way that they become assets. At any rate, being aware of them has the potential to enhance both the quality of your interactions with others as well as your happiness.

What Makes an ISFJ Happy?

The ISFJ type is known for its wariness and has even been described as pessimistic before. This outlook on life however, is simply an attempt to make sure that chances for happiness are available to all, including you. Indeed, it can be said that the ability to provide these opportunities is the basis for finding your own joy in life.

As a child, you can be trusted to follow the rules of the classroom. While other types may spend their time pushing boundaries or looking for their place in all of the chaos, you will simply look to the teacher for guidance. Even at a young age, structure will make you feel at ease, a need that will remain as you get older.

In school, you enjoy taking courses that deal with business and economics. The humanities, sciences, and arts are not of much interest to you because they are not likely to contribute to your ability to provide for yourself and those around you. Once they have finished their studies, each personality type forms their own working style that includes the "material" they prefer to deal with, as well as a specific approach. While the more idealistic types are happiest working with people and using their empathetic listening skills, ISFJ's are content to manage "things." You find the opportunity to gather, organize, distribute and keep track of the supplies in the job description your ideal vocation.[28] The right job can be instrumental when it comes to having a positive self-image, particularly for you.

Your self-image is based on your idea of success, which is not only dependent on the way you see yourself, but also how you feel others see you. If you can successfully portray yourself as trustworthy, responsible, and altruistic, then your self-esteem will be at its highest. You are a natural Good Samaritan who can often be found volunteering in soup kitchens, helping out at your church, or distributing toys and food to children in need. Your hard work touches the lives of many, but even you need a break now and then. On those extremely rare occasions when you take a vacation, you are more than delighted to leave behind your responsibilities and fill the role of the receiver, instead of the giver. Lounging at the beach or visiting a spa is not your style, however. Instead, your time will be scheduled to provide you with lots of chances to visit historical sites and take guided tours.[29]

When you get back from vacation, you will immediately return to your duties feeling refreshed and ready to work. ISFJ's always put forth their best effort and it makes you feel appreciated when you are recognized with certificates or other types of physical rewards. This is particularly beneficial for your self-esteem since you prefer for your achievements to speak for themselves and normally would not call attention to them directly. Despite this modesty, when you walk into an ISFJ's office or home, you may see a corner or small display tastefully arranged with photos of their family and awards they have won.

Being recognized can also contribute to your yearning for belonging. It is not uncommon to find the name of an ISFJ on several club rosters; that is, clubs whose primary mission is to assist in the community. The need to know that you have done everything possible to be an upstanding and contributing member of society is quite considerable. These memberships also give you a person, place, or cause to provide your personal loyalty to.[30]

When it comes to your family and friends, you will toil alongside both to build the life that you believe they should have. There is no prouder parent than an ISFJ who has raised their offspring to be independent and law-abiding members of society. You will be thrilled to share your accomplishments with the close friends you have made over the years, whose friendships provide you with a deep, emotional bond to them. The same can be said for your relationship with your spouse. ISFJ's are very romantic and will search for someone who deserves their unconditional love and nurturing.

Your personality type's happiness is generally dependent on your ability to be useful. Most of the time you accomplish this marvelously, and some of the biggest contributors to society have been ISFJ's. Taking your desires and talents into account when it comes to your daily life will guide you on the path towards both success and happiness.

What are Some Common Careers of an ISFJ?

ISFJ's satisfaction is partly based on finding a career that will give them the opportunity to utilize their skills to the best of their ability. Your chosen vocation should be one in which you can serve others in some capacity, yet it must also provide the structure and rules that you crave. Your type is lucky in that you can enjoy both working alone and with others.[31] A need for job security will also lead you to more traditional careers that deal with the tangible instead of the abstract.

Your preference for providing aid to others makes you an obvious fit for many helping fields. Jobs where you can interact with clients or patients one-on-one and see the positive impact that your work has on them are ideal. Your pleasant persona will also allow you to work with any age group. Since your type has a need to protect specifically, you often make excellent social workers. Your encyclopedic memory and social skills also ensure that you will enjoy a career as a family doctor, nurse, or physical therapist.[32]

Several surveys found that ISFJ's flock to teaching as well, particularly when it comes to the preschool and elementary ages. This can be explained by your appreciation for strong tradition and enjoyment of the nurturing aspect of teaching. When working with students at these age levels, you will enjoy having the time to focus on teaching basic skills that require attention to details. Other educational positions that have similar responsibilities include speech-language pathologists and teachers of special education students.[33]

Since you also tend to enjoy the past and its preservation, you are likely to be found working as a curator. There is no question that you will meet every deadline without fail and your endless amount of patience and perfectionism will assist you in interpreting works of art with a thoroughness that other types cannot. You may also enjoy working as a librarian, where you can be of service to the public directly. These two jobs also give the ISFJ opportunities to use their excellent organizational and recollection skills.

Although you enjoy teamwork at times, it is much more likely that you will take a technical job if you can work independently. Such vocations might include photography or a career as an electrician. These careers will be most gratifying, due to the opportunities you have to use refined skills and experience significant and meaningful interactions with customers. Since you prefer to stay in the background, working in a corporate environment is much less appealing to you. Again, if this were to occur, a high level of independence would be required. Two examples of this type of environment include human resources or a position as an administrative assistant.[34]

When it comes to artistic careers, ISFJ's must carefully consider the areas in which their skills can be effectively used. Although artistic talent can be common in your type, you are better off using it practically instead of in areas like the fine arts. With your ability to create an aesthically pleasing environment, you may find that you enjoy interior or fashion design very much. Since you are particularly affected by your own home's design, it is quite easy for you to understand your client's need to live in a comfortable and attractive home.

It is very clear that as an ISFJ, you have many career choices available to you. Once you begin working in a chosen vocation, it is not uncommon for you to rise through the ranks quickly by using your diverse skills.

Common Workplace Behaviors of an ISFJ

When working in a chosen vocation, ISFJ'S tend to display certain behaviors in the workplace regardless of the setting. For example, your love of rules will ensure that you will read the employee handbook from cover to cover and be inspired to follow its contents religiously.

No one will ever have to worry about any impulsivity on your part and because of this you are often described as extremely dependable, patient, and thorough. When approaching a problem or task, the first step you always take is to look at all of the given facts. Only then, will you decide if and what type of action should be taken. Also, playing a part in the decision-making process are your past experiences and moral code. However, it is important to note that while other personality types are interested in making others feel better about them, you tend to focus more on determining whether an action is right or wrong. Your Judging (J) trait means that you consider any decisions you make to be final, as opposed to open-ended.[35]

Tasks that emphasize working with or thinking about possibilities can make your sensible and down-to-earth personality uncomfortable. You would much rather work with facts and cold, hard evidence. As an employee, you usually do not enjoy thinking about new ways to solve old issues or exploring possible directions for the company's future.

The introverted quality of your type allows you to work on one project for an extended period of time without breaks. Since you work so hard, you may be the first to get to the office and the last to leave as well. As an ISFJ, you will need a plan before you start to work. Therefore, it is not unusual to walk into your office and see more than one To-Do list hanging on the wall. You will meticulously follow that schedule and proceed step-by-step when completing a task.[36]

Given your preference for such lists, it should not be shocking that you are likely to be unhappy with any type of surprise. Advance warning can help soften the blow but a change that would, for example, cut back on funding for customer service or completely change a well-established routine can be very distressing to you.

Despite your practical nature, ISFJ's are usually very talented when it comes to observing and being aware of other people's feelings. You are often described as tactful and are genuinely concerned for the welfare of others. You take everyone's needs into account, sometimes at the expense of your own. Conflict terrifies you and you'll avoid saying anything that could be construed as unpleasant or cause friction.[37] If it can't be helped, then the best way to resolve conflict is to meet alone and discuss the topic of disagreement.

This way, both parties can agree on a way that the work can be done that pleases both of them.

It is safe to say then that office politics are of no interest to ISFJ's. With your introversion and desire for a harmonious working environment, volunteering for a leadership position will not be high on your radar. Having said, if an ISFJ were forced or convinced to take on such a position, then their performance will be more than adequate. As a boss, you are sure to be consistent in what you say and will expect your employees to follow the same policies that you do. It is important to note that your high standards often mean that you end up doing all of the work yourself, instead of delegating it! For this reason, ISFJ's may often be overworked, although you would never know it, given that displays of emotion are rare.[38]

Even though they have the mentality of "If you want it done right, do it yourself," ISFJ's love to know that their hard work is appreciated by others. This can be very difficult for others to discover though, since they never brag about their accomplishments. This attitude and your dependability can sometimes mean that you are overlooked for promotions or taken for granted.

Thanks to your people skills, reliability, and dedication to your work, your type is often seen as a model employee. These same qualities make you a wonderful friend, family member, or significant other as well.

ISFJs and Personal Relationships

When it comes to your priority list, your personal relationships are at the top. You get along best with people who have personalities and values similar to yours and your big heart guides you to believe that you can bring out the best in people. Thanks to your sensitivity to others' feelings and wish for harmony, you often have an innate ability to accomplish this goal.

ISFJ's are usually content with having a few, close friends whose company they can enjoy over a lifetime. Most would say that when it comes to these friendships, you prefer quality over quantity. Your extreme loyalty (and dislike of conflict) means that you will drop everything and run to a friend's side if need be. You are likely to be very generous with your time and may even have a hard time saying no (although this applies to most relationships in your life, whether personal or business). When faced with any kind of conflict, your goal is to get as far away as possible in the shortest amount of time. Still, even though your friends may not be able to count on you fighting alongside or with them, they can rest assured that you will find someone with the proper authority who can settle the disagreement at hand.

As mentioned earlier, your thoughtfulness and creativity when it comes to gift-giving also sets you apart from other types. There is room for improvement in this area however, in that there may be times you give the recipient what you think they should want, instead of what they actually do.[39]

Another reason your social circle may be small is your fear of vulnerability. ISFJ's are highly sensitive, especially when it comes to criticism from those they trust and/or respect. Therefore, sharing your feelings is not often on your immediate list of things to do. Your need for privacy may lead some to believe that your feelings are shallow in some way or that they simply do not exist. This could not be further from the truth! Your inner world is very rich and the intensity of your emotions is greater than anyone would guess. Only those you trust will have the opportunity to see and hear about your passion and zest for life as you speak in endless detail about the events you are presently experiencing.

Your attempts at hiding your reactions and emotions do not necessarily promise a capability for it. It is not unusual for those who do not know you well to find themselves bewildered by your sudden moodiness. In almost all cases, your attitude is due to a misguided attempt not to burden others with your more negative emotions.[40]

One of the most important partnerships in your life is the one you have with your spouse. You find an indescribable joy in providing support to your loved one and do not take the matter of dating lightly. One-night stands are not for you and you are looking for the one who truly means it when they say, "'Til death do us part". Environments that lend themselves to conversations on a deeper level or places that breed familiarity will be the most beneficial for your dating life. You will tend to be most attracted to those who share your Sensing (S) trait. Some research also notes that those who possess one or two opposing traits will also be appealing, but it is essential that you look at each potential mate on a case-by-case basis. ISFJ's are known to have some of the highest rates for dissatisfaction in their partnerships.[41]

Relationships with your children are likely to be positive, at least during the younger years when they look to you for guidance. Your vast amounts of patience will be helpful as you navigate the years that are characterized by boundary testing. As they age, more independent children may experience your unconditional love and concern as stifling. The opposite can also occur, with those who are dependent finding it difficult to carve a path for themselves without your help. In general, you are open-minded when it comes to your children's differences and will accept them even if you do not understand them.

The connections you make with your family, friends, and partner have a special meaning to you as an ISFJ. With the support and love of these people by your side, you will find the strength to achieve whatever you set out to accomplish.

ISFJ: Parenting Style and Values

Parenting comes naturally to ISFJ types, thanks to your desire to nurture. Any children you have will be sure to grow up in a stable environment with plenty of love and support. Your patience will also ensure that your children have ample opportunities to safely explore their surroundings.

When angry, ISFJ parents will not be the type to raise their voices. Ordinarily, you are soft-spoken and gentle, but you will still rule your home with a traditional fist. The phrase "free-spirited" does not describe you and some might label you as a "helicopter" parent. When it comes to raising your children, you assume that what worked well in the past should have the same effect in the present. It will be important to you to clearly define your role as the parent in your child's eyes and you will not be accused of trying to be their friend. As with their own lives, ISFJ parents expect their children to follow the rules laid out by society. With your sons, you may be a bit more relaxed when it comes to mischief and you may even be able to find the humor in certain instances. When it comes to your daughters, however, tradition is more likely to be upheld.[42]

As with all of your relationships, confrontation is an issue for your personality type, even with your own children. When their children misbehave, ISFJ parents can be uncomfortable with meting out punishment. This does not mean that there will be a lack of discipline, however. Since order and structure is so important to you, you are usually able to overcome your discomfort and provide the well-defined boundaries that your children need. When they come of age, you expect that they will become conscientious and productive members of society. If for some reason they do not, you can take it quite personally, believing that you went wrong somewhere in the rearing process.[43]

On a more positive note, affection is never lacking with an ISFJ parent. With your excellent memory and attention to detail, it is common for your type to know about and attempt to provide all of the little things that make your child happy. You make sure the household is always running smoothly, for the benefit of all of your family members. They can expect that you will provide them with nutritious meals, as well as a clean and orderly home. You will not expect much, if anything, for these services, but a little bit of appreciation can go a long way in lifting your spirits.

With that in mind, you can be quite possessive when it comes to your family members and may feel easily rejected in certain circumstances. One such instance can occur if your clan consists of extroverted members who prefer to socialize outside of the family. Similar feelings may come up with introverted family members who are more comfortable keeping to themselves as well.

Your instincts give you an edge when it comes to raising well-adjusted and responsible adults, especially when compared to other Myers-Briggs types. The relationships you have with each family member will be full of love and concern, thanks to your constant consideration of their happiness. Because of this, many of your personal relationships are likely to run just as smoothly.

Why Do ISFJs Make Good Friends?

As with their other relationships, ISFJ's will give plenty of affection and support to their friends. However, it can take time for you to open up to others. Although many may call the ISFJ a friend, being called a friend back by this type is a rare occurrence indeed. You are very protective of your emotions and need to connect on a deeper emotional level. For this reason, it is unusual for you to make friends through nights out at bars and clubs (places you are unlikely to go to anyway), but through activities where you may see the same people multiple times and can get to know them little by little. You may meet these people in places such as work or in class. Like most introverts, the ISFJ usually only has a few close friends.

Your type is likely to place your family above your friends in terms of priority. Nevertheless, any time spent with your friends will still be valued and cherished. You love to talk things over before you make decisions, but only with those you trust. With them, you may agonize over the details of previous decisions or talk about the present happenings in your life. With others however, you are much more reserved, which can make you come across as cold and uncaring.

The ISFJ friend can be needy at times and the way a potential friend reacts to this display of emotions will either ensure the survival of the friendship or threaten it. As you become closer to your friends, there is a good chance that you will put their needs above your own. You may go out of their way to support them or have a hard time refusing them. If a friend is in need, the ISFJ will not need to be asked for help. You will meet with and actively assist them in trying to solve their problem. If their efforts are not reciprocated, you may feel disappointed and may even hold a grudge. It may be difficult to tell though, since you will not air your feelings in an attempt to avoid conflict.

Normally you are very respectful and accepting of your friends' differences and are not picky about the personality types you will hang around. When discussing important matters, you may seek out an Intuitive (N) friend. With them, you have the opportunity to deliberate over matters of the heart and you enjoy the wisdom and advice that these acquaintances can give you. Most of your other friends, however, are more similar to you, which may give you a better chance of avoiding miscommunication. Therefore, your type is most likely to have ISFJ or ESFJ friends.

Within all of your friendships, your sensitivity, need for harmony, and exceptional recollection skills allow you to make them feel unique.[44] No birthday or anniversary will ever be forgotten and every special occasion will be made memorable with a gift tailored to their personality.

ISFJ's are committed to their friendships and cherish those that can stand the test of time the most. Your affection and concern for your friends' well-being make you one of the best personality types to befriend, although getting to know you can be quite difficult. These characteristics can also carry over into your romantic relationships.

ISFJ Romance

When it comes to romantic relationships, there is no other area in which the ISFJ will strive to create the most balance. Your type takes dating very seriously. You expect your partners to be monogamous and will give them the same courtesy.

Married and otherwise committed ISFJ's make wonderful homemakers. You will take your duties seriously and will work to make sure the laundry is washed, pressed, and folded promptly. In addition, homemade dinners will be a regular occurrence and the house will always be neat and tidy. The male ISFJ's will follow their self-appointed traditional male role just as sincerely. It is only right that you are the primary breadwinner. On the weekends, you can be found tinkering around the house, fixing anything broken and making sure your yard is presentable. These actions are but a small glimpse into your devotion to your partner, but it is important to keep in mind that emotional needs must also be met.[45]

Your shyness and reluctance to express your feelings at any stage of the relationship can have a negative effect on it. Over time, your partner may learn that asking you directly about your feelings is the best way to get you to share. Most of the time, however, you will express your love through actions, which tend to be thoughtful and caring.

As with all of your relationships, you will often put your partner's needs above your own. This can have tragic effects, particularly if you are with someone who is willing to take advantage of you. In this case, you may find that your relationship can take a toll on your health when you do not express your irritation and annoyance. There are many instances of ISFJ's allowing their resentment to fester until they explode. When this finally occurs, you may say things that you regret later.

When compared to other types, you have a difficult time leaving a romantic relationship or accepting that one is over. Your tendency to shoulder responsibility for the success of a relationship often leads to you blaming yourself when it does not work out. You will often spend a lot of time after the fact considering whether the decisions you made were the right ones. In fact, your loyalty is so strong that sometimes you are faithful to your deceased partners for the rest of your life.

The ESFP and the ESTP can be wonderful partners for you. These types share your need to view life with a practical outlook, yet they can also encourage you to strengthen their social abilities and decision-making skills. On the other side, you can inspire these partners to limit the amount of time they take before making a decision and learn to enjoy time spent alone. Your sensitivity makes those with Feeling (F) traits more attractive to you as well. Keep in mind that though you tend to prefer those who are more similar to you than not, you may do just as well with another ISFJ.[46]

When we delve more deeply into your potential romantic relationships, we can see that the combination of an extrovert and introvert can sometimes be a difficult one. Myers-Briggs explained in her book *Gifts Differing: Understanding Personality Type* that an extroverted type is more aware of what people are truly like, thanks to the opportunities they have had to socialize with a variety of people. Therefore, he or she may be able to make a more informed choice about the person they marry. This indicates that you should be more careful than others in matters of love, particularly when it comes to choosing your mate.

It may be obvious to some that an introvert and extrovert have very different tolerance levels when it comes to sociability. This can, and does, have a negative effect on the relationship at times. When the

65

ISFJ works at a socially demanding job, the effects can be even greater. If your partner does not understand your need for quiet, there may be frustration on both of your parts.[47]

Although many successful relationships consist of a partner with a Thinking (T) characteristic and a Feeling (F) trait, this combination can have its issues. When the former is objective and forthcoming with criticism, the latter (in this case, the ISFJ) will feel hurt and betrayed. In any case, respect for your partner's differences and compromise will be essential components of a successful relationship.

7 Actionable Steps for Overcoming Your Weaknesses as an ISFJ

When you have recognized and are ready to change your habits, where do you start? This list is not exhaustive by any means, but the following steps can help you attain a healthier and more confident persona:

1. Widen Your Perspective

Having a more accurate picture of what is really in front of you can be beneficial in determining what your next step should be in many circumstances. When you take in foreign information from a variety of sources that you would not normally acknowledge, you begin to realize that there is a place in your well-ordered world for varying opinions and outcomes.[48]

2. Consider the Validity of Others' Feelings

Remember that the feelings and values others have are unique and valuable to them. This may seem like an obvious concept, but it can be one that ISFJ's ignore in certain situations. You may feel that your thoughts and emotions behind an idea negate those of another, although you would probably never admit it. Consider this: do you only value input from those who agree with you or your cause? Or do you attempt to truly understand their motives without judgment? Pay close attention to your thoughts to determine whether you are ignoring their contributions simply because they do not fit into your notions of what should be.[49]

3. Attempt to Allow Others to Take the Lead

If there is a nine page to-do list, the ISFJ will hunker down and attempt to complete every task solo. This will occur despite having a 10-man team at your disposal. Your sense of duty and wish to remain in control can prevent you from even considering the idea that you are not the only one who can get the job done. You should recognize that when you allow others to help you, you are affirming that they have the necessary talents, as well as your trust, to help you. Even if you only delegate one or two tasks out of thirty, it is a step in the right direction.

4. Let Your True Feelings Be Known

ISFJ's take great care when it comes to considering the feelings of others. This is a feat for which you should be congratulated! Your issue lies in the fact that you do not give yourself the same courtesy when it comes to your own feelings. Allowing your emotions to build up to the point where there is physical tension and illness present in your life can have a grave effect on your relationships and ability to help others. Recognize that there are many healthy ways to express emotions that will not lead to confrontation, such as writing a letter or sticking to specifics when discussing the issue ("You're always late!" becomes "Yesterday, I asked you to meet me at 8 and you didn't show up until 8:30.").

5. Don't Take Things So Personally

The lack of this tactic in your life is a large part of why you fear conflict as an ISFJ. To you, every interaction you have can be categorized as very personal. You should keep in mind that others may not feel the same way about the depth of your conversations. They may not wish for their words to imply that you are not capable or be construed as criticism. Many times they are merely suggestions. Your memory and ability to hold a grudge may prevent you from hearing the true meaning of their words. Remind yourself that objectivity is a trait that is needed in everyone, including you.[50]

6. Look into the Future-Not the Past

It has been well documented that the ISFJ prefers to live in the past. Real change can frighten them, a reaction that is common in many types. However, consider that those who look to the future tend to be more successful professionally and academically.[51]

Although daydreaming is frowned upon by some, it is a tool of many future-oriented people. Try doing some of your own and your hope and excitement for what is to come may begin to outweigh your longing for what was.

7. Stop the Pessimism

For some reason, ISFJ's tend to expect the worst in most situations. Your tendency for pessimism often stems from your attempts to be prepared for everything and your fear of what will happen if you are not. Accept that this will not always be possible and explore what would happen if you were caught unprepared (hypothetically, of course). Consider that the outcome may not be as bad as you think. Keep in mind that changing this outlook may take quite a while, so it is important to be patient!

The 10 Most Influential ISFJs We Can Learn From

1. Mother Teresa

As one of the most selfless and caring people of the 21st century, Mother Teresa's main focus in life was to serve and protect the disadvantaged. Her ISFJ nature was instrumental in guiding her on her path of sacrifice and honest work. The tenacity and compassion she showed proves that no amount of kindness is too small to make an impact.

2. Jimmy Carter

As an ISFJ, Jimmy Carter has always had the natural inclination to overlook and accept the differences present in others, even in times when it would have benefited him to do just the opposite. During the Civil Rights era, he affirmed its importance by hiring African-Americans and keeping portraits of them in an office that attracted the KKK several times. Presently, he still uses his influence for a number of conflict resolution, human rights, and charitable causes.[52] Carter has truly embodied the ISFJ tendency to stand up for those who cannot do it themselves through his actions.

3. Rosa Parks

One of the most famous civil rights figures, Rosa Parks was a quiet and introverted woman who saw the injustice of segregation even as a young child. After her fateful bus ride one afternoon in 1955, she continued to be an instrumental part of the civil rights movement, despite being fired from her job and receiving death threats.[53] Her lifelong fight to make her voice heard proves that courage can be found in all types of people.

4. J.P. Morgan

Morgan's company, the J.P. Morgan & Company firm, had a knack for taking troubled businesses and reorganizing them. Morgan's aid to the government also helped end or lessen the effects of two recessions in the U.S.[54] It can be said that he explored and demonstrated the importance of strategy, a talent that is present in many ISFJ's.

5. Prince Charles

The son of Queen Elizabeth II, Prince Charles has used his influence to help others in need, as many ISFJ's do. He established The Prince's Trust in 1976 to provide mentoring support and financial grants to disadvantaged youth, along with 16 other charitable organizations.[55] The concern and philanthropy that he has shown and provided for others displays the good that can come of benevolent leading.

6. Johnny Carson

As a child, Carson took it upon himself to learn magic tricks and performed shows for the community. As an adult, he charmed audiences nationwide on The

Tonight Show and made otherwise drab guests appear to be funny and exciting. From him, we can learn about the importance of sociability and charisma.

7. Louisa May Alcott

One of the most prolific female writers of her time, Louisa May Alcott wrote to escape the poverty of her family and pressure of the jobs she took to support them. She served as a nurse during the American Civil War and the letters she sent home were recognized for their observations and humor. Her most famous work, *Little Women*, was a semi-autobiographical account of her childhood.[56] Her creativity and ability to make the best out of tough situations should be remembered by all.

8. Warren Buffet

Even as a child, Warren Buffett showed an interest in making and saving money. He worked a variety of small jobs, such as selling chewing gum, delivering newspapers, and detailing cars. By age 20, he had made and saved $9,800 (over $96,000 today); by 1958, that figure was over $174,000 ($1.47 million today). The ease with which he manages finances is a talent found frequently in ISFJ's. Buffett's actions show how important it can be to learn about the value of money and investment.

9. Kristi Yamaguchi

Yamaguchi began taking ice-skating and ballet lessons as a child as physical therapy for her club feet. She went on to win many titles, including 2 World Figure Skating Championships in 1991 and 1992 and a U.S. Figure Skating Championship in 1992. She is also the 1992 Olympic Champion in ladies' singles.[57] The perseverance Yamaguchi showed should be a lesson that hard work is essential in achieving our dreams.

10. Tiger Woods

Described as one of the most successful golfers of all time, Tiger Woods was a child prodigy, being introduced to golf before the age of two by his father Earl. By 11 years old, his father could no longer win a game against him despite his best efforts. As of 2014, he has won 79 official PGA Tour events including 14 majors.[58] Tiger's background demonstrates the fact that when one has determination it can open up the opportunities we need to become successful.

Conclusion

As an ISFJ, you are unique among the Myers-Briggs personality types. There is no other type who has the ability to serve and protect so many in need. Your unique way of viewing the world and its people illuminate paths to a more humane and efficient world that are hidden to most.

Your personality allows you to straddle the line between Introvert (I) and Extrovert (E), a rare quality indeed. Take advantage of this trait by pairing it with the more than adequate social skills you possess to bring the two groups closer. Your Sensing (S) trait has provided you with the practicality that comes along with being realistic and you feel at home in the world as it is now. Your Feeling (F) sensibilities offset this Sensing (S) trait in that you are able to understand the importance of compassion. Finally, as a Judging (J) type, your responsibility and self-discipline have no limits. Paying attention to these personality attributes will assist you in discovering ways to enhance your life as a whole.

The career you choose can have a great effect on you and the lives of others. Pick positions where your quiet tenacity and empathy will be an asset. You would also do well to have more confidence in your leadership abilities, as well as in your colleagues. You can be very inspiring with your ability to complete what may seem like daunting tasks but you must realize that you will not be considered weak if you ask for help.

Although you may feel that it is wrong to want recognition for your achievements, you should realize that the role you play in the lives of others cannot be filled by anyone else. Owning up to what you have accomplished will only serve to increase your capable reputation in the eyes of your teammates. Your emotions and your health will also be much more stable if you acknowledge that your needs and wants are just as important as those you serve.

Your personal relationships play a large role in your happiness. The intrinsic ability you have to accurately sense and recognize the moods and emotions of others should not be taken for granted. It is a rare talent to possess and its presence can guide you to some truly wonderful experiences with those you love and cherish.

ISFJ's of the past and present have proven that success can be attained through a combination of selflessness, tenacity, and empathy. From golf players to presidents, you can excel in nearly every arena of life when you learn to use your talents for good. Since this comes naturally to you, there will likely be many more ISFJ's whose societal contributions change the world.

It is up to you to recognize and develop your talents. You should remember that your innate talent for assessing the harmony and balance of a situation can be very helpful when it comes to personal development. With your willingness to work hard, success is inevitable for you.

Final Word/About the Author

I was born and raised in Norwalk, Connecticut. Growing up, I could often be found spending afternoons reading in the local public library about management techniques and leadership styles, along with overall outlooks towards life. It was from spending those afternoons reading about how others have led productive lives that I was inspired to start studying patterns of human behavior and self-improvement. Usually I write works around sports to learn more about influential athletes in the hopes that from my writing, you the reader can walk away inspired to put in an equal if not greater amount of hard work and perseverance to pursue your goals. However, I began writing about psychology topics such as the Myers Brigg Type Indicator so that I could help others better understand why they act and think the way they do and how to build on their strengths while also identifying their weaknesses. If you enjoyed

ISFJ: Understanding & Relating with the Protector please leave a review! Also, you can read more of my works on *How to be Witty, How to be Likeable, Bargain Shopping, Productivity Hacks, Morning Meditation, Becoming a Father,* and *33 Life Lessons: Success Principles, Career Advice & Habits of Successful People* in the Kindle Store.

Like what you read?

If you love books on life, basketball, or productivity, check out my website at claytongeoffreys.com to join my exclusive list where I let you know about my latest books. Aside from being the first to hear about my latest releases, you can also download a free copy of *33 Life Lessons: Success Principles, Career Advice & Habits of Successful People.* See you there!

[1]Briggs Myers, Isabel. & McCaulley, Mary H. "Chapter 1." *Manual: A Guide to the Development and Use of the Myers-Briggs Type Indicator®*. 5th ed. Palo Alto: Consulting Psychologists Press, 1989. 1-2. Print.

[2] Briggs Myers, I. & McCaulley, M.H. 1-2. Print.

[3] Briggs Myers, I. & McCaulley, M.H. 1-2. Print.

[4] Briggs Myers, I. & McCaulley, M.H. 12-14. Print.

[5] Briggs Myers, I. & McCaulley, M.H. 12-14. Print.

[6] Briggs Myers, I. & McCaulley, M.H. 12-14. Print.

[7] Briggs Myers, I. & McCaulley, M.H. 12-14. Print.

[8] Briggs Myers, I. & McCaulley, M.H. 12-14. Print.

[9] Briggs Myers, I. & McCaulley, M.H. 12-14. Print.

[10]Briggs Myers, I. & McCaulley, M.H. 12-14. Print.

[11]Briggs Myers, I. & McCaulley, M.H. 12-14. Print.

[12]"Frequently Asked Questions." *MBTItoday*. N.p., n.d. Web.

[13]"Ways Type Can Be Used." *The Myers & Briggs Foundation*. N.p, n.d. Web.

[14]"What Can I Do With My Personality Type? ISFJ Careers and Majors." *Ball State University.* N.p., n.d. Web.

[15]Brightman, Harvey J. "GSU Master Teaching Program: On Learning Styles." *Georgia State University.* N.p., 2013. Web.

[16]Keirsey, David. "Guardian Role Variants-The Protector." *Please Understand Me II: Temperament, Character, Intelligence.* 1st ed. Del-Mar: Prometheus Nemesis Book Company, 1998. 45. Print.

[17]"ISFJ Personality." *16 Personalities.* N.p., n.d. Web.

[18]Keirsey, David. 95. Print.

[19]"Guardian™ Portrait of the Protector: ISFJ." *Keirsey.* N.p., n.d. Web.

[20]Keirsey, David. 114. Print.

[21]"ISFJ Personality." *16 Personalities.* N.p., n.d. Web.

[22]Keirsey, David. 114. Print.

[23]"ISFJ Personality." *16 Personalities.* N.p., n.d. Web.

[24]"ISFJ Leadership: Leading Self and Others."

Personality Central. N.p., July 2014. Web.

[25]"ISFJ Personality." *16 Personalities.* N.p., n.d. Web.

[26]Keirsey, David. 113. Print.

[27]"ISFJ Personality." *16 Personalities.* N.p., n.d. Web.

[28]Keirsey, David. 88. Print.

[29]Keirsey, David. 96. Print.

[30] Keirsey, David. 98. Print.

[31]Keirsey, David. 113. Print.

[32]Briggs Myers, Isabel and Myers, Peter B.
"Introverted Sensing Types." *Gifts Differing: Understanding Personality Type. "* 1st ed. Palo Alto: Davies-Black Publishing, 1995. 104. Print.

[33]Rushton, Stephen, Morgan, Jackson, and Richard, Michael."Teacher's Myers-Briggs personality profiles: Identifying effective teacher personality traits." *Teaching and Teacher Education* 23 (2007): 437-439. ScienceDirect. University of South Florida. Web.

[34]"Guardian™ Portrait of the Protector: ISFJ." *Keirsey.*

[35]Keirsey, David. 88. Print.

[36]Krebs Hirsh, Sandra A. and Kummerow, Jean M.
"ISFJ: Introverted Sensing with Feeling."
Introduction to Type in Organizations. 3rd ed. Palo
Alto: Consulting Psychologists Press, 1993. 14. Print.

[37]Krebs Hirsh, Sandra A. and Kummerow, Jean M. 14.
Print.

[38]"ISFJ Personality." *16 Personalities.* N.p., n.d. Web.

[39]"ISFJ." *David Markley.* N.p, n.d. Web.

[40]"ISFJ." *David Markley.* N.p, n.d. Web.

[41]"ISFJ Personality." *16 Personalities.* N.p., n.d. Web.

[42]Keirsey, David. 113. Print.

[43]"ISFJ Relationships." *Personality Page.* N.p., n.d.
Web.

[44]"ISFJ." *David Markley.* N.p, n.d. Web.

[45]Keirsey, David. 114. Print.

[46]"ISFJ Personality." *16 Personalities.* N.p., n.d. Web.

[47]Briggs Myers, Isabel and Myers, Peter B. 124. Print.

[48]ISFJ Development." *16 Personalities.* N.p., n.d.

Web.

[49]ISFJ Development." *16 Personalities.* N.p., n.d.
Web.

[50]"ISFJ Personality." *16 Personalities.* N.p., n.d. Web.

[51]Immerwahr, John. "Different Time Perspectives."
Teach Philosophy 101. N.p., May 16,2012. Web.

[52]"Jimmy Carter." *Wikipedia.* N.p., n.d. Web.

[53]"Rosa Parks." *Wikipedia.* N.p., n.d. Web.

[54]"J.P. Morgan." *Wikipedia.* N.p., n.d. Web.

[55]"Prince Charles." *Wikipedia.* N.p., n.d. Web.

[56]"Louisa May Alcott." *Wikipedia.* N.p., n.d. Web.

[57]"Kristi Yamaguchi." *Wikipedia.* N.p., n.d. Web.

[58]"Tiger Woods." *Wikipedia.* N.p., n.d. Web.

Printed in Great Britain
by Amazon

36051785R00056